ALL THIS
AND SNOOPY,
TOO

THE PEANUTS GALLERY

includes:

IT'S YOUR TURN, SNOOPY   2-4061-4 $1.25
(selected cartoons from *You're The Guest Of Honor, Charlie Brown*, Vol. 1)

THAT'S LIFE, SNOOPY   2-3876-8 $1.25
(selected cartoons from *Thompson Is In Trouble, Charlie Brown*, Vol 2)

YOU'VE COME A LONG WAY,
SNOOPY   2-4004-5 $1.25
(selected cartoons from *Thompson Is In Trouble, Charlie Brown*, Vol. 1)

YOU'VE GOT TO BE YOU,
SNOOPY   2-3774-5 $1.25
(selected cartoons from *You've Come A Long Way, Charlie Brown*, Vol. 2)

ALL THIS AND SNOOPY, TOO

Selected Cartoons from
YOU CAN'T WIN, CHARLIE BROWN
VOL 1

By CHARLES M. SCHULZ

FAWCETT CREST • NEW YORK

ALL THIS AND SNOOPY, TOO

This book, prepared especially for Fawcett Crest Books, a unit of CBS Publications, the Consumer Publishing Division of CBS Inc., comprises the first half of YOU CAN'T WIN, CHARLIE BROWN, and is reprinted by arrangement with Holt, Rinehart and Winston, Inc.

ISBN: 0-449-23824-5

Printed in the United States of America

43   42   41   40   39   38   37   36

THIS BLANKET ABSORBS ALL MY FEARS AND FRUSTRATIONS

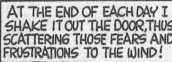

AT THE END OF EACH DAY I SHAKE IT OUT THE DOOR, THUS SCATTERING THOSE FEARS AND FRUSTRATIONS TO THE WIND!

WHAT ABOUT TOMORROW?

TOMORROW I START WITH A CLEAN BLANKET

NOT UNLIKE THE PROVERBIAL CLEAN SLATE!

LOOK, CHARLIE BROWN.. YOU HAVE FEARS AND YOU HAVE FRUSTRATIONS... AM I RIGHT?

OF COURSE, I'M RIGHT! SO WHAT YOU NEED IS A BLANKET LIKE THIS TO SOAK UP THOSE FEARS AND FRUSTRATIONS!

I DON'T KNOW...

I THINK MOST OF LIFE'S PROBLEMS ARE TOO COMPLICATED TO BE SOLVED WITH A SPIRITUAL BLOTTER!

WHAT'S THIS ABOUT MISS OTHMAR COMING BACK?

SHE **IS**, CHARLIE BROWN! SHE'S COMING BACK TO OUR SCHOOL TO TEACH AGAIN!

I THOUGHT HER NAME WAS MRS. HAGEMEYER NOW...

NO, THAT'S JUST HER MARRIED NAME...

IN **REAL** LIFE SHE'S MISS OTHMAR!

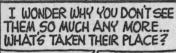

I NEVER KNOW WHAT TO DO WITH THE USED TEA BAG..

IT ALWAYS SEEMS SO QUIET AROUND HERE ON THE DAY HE GOES TO VISIT HIS GRANDFATHER...

NOT REALLY... BUT I GET FIFTEEN CENTS A WEEK FOR FEEDING THE DOG..

WELL! THAT MAKES ME FEEL KIND OF IMPORTANT...

BY CREATING WORK, I AM HELPING TO BOLSTER OUR ECONOMY!

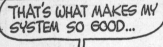

ALL OF EARTH'S CREATURES HAVE, HIDDEN WITHIN THEIR BEINGS, A WILD UNCONTROLLABLE URGE TO PUNT!

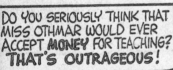

OH, MISS OTHMAR, HOW COULD YOU?

I THOUGHT YOU WERE TEACHING US BECAUSE YOU LOVED US! I NEVER DREAMED YOU WERE GETTING PAID FOR IT!

WAIT A MINUTE! MAYBE SHE'S GETTING PAID, BUT YET NOT REALLY ACCEPTING THE MONEY!

I'LL BET THAT'S IT! I'LL BET SHE'S TURNING IT ALL BACK IN! OH, MISS OTHMAR, YOU'RE A TRUE GEM!!

BY THE TIME I'M EIGHTEEN, I EXPECT THIS WORLD TO BE PERFECT!

WHY SHOULD I HAVE TO LIVE IN A WORLD SOMEBODY ELSE HAS MESSED UP?! I'LL GIVE THEM TWELVE YEARS TO GET EVERYTHING IN ORDER!

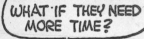

WHAT IF THEY NEED MORE TIME?

TELL THEM NOT TO BOTHER WIRING FOR AN EXTENSION... THE ANSWER WILL BE, "NO!"

WHEN YOU'RE ON YOUR WAY TO SCHOOL, AND YOU MEET A DOG, YOU SHOULD ALWAYS STOP, AND PAT HIM ON THE HEAD...

PAT PAT

THAT ALWAYS GETS YOUR DAY OFF TO A GOOD START..

WELL, AT LEAST I'M CONTRIBUTING SOMETHING TO SOCIETY!

GOOD GRIEF! HERE COMES LUCY! I'M TRAPPED!

SHE SAID SHE'D THROW MY BLANKET IN THE TRASH BURNER THE NEXT TIME SHE SAW IT....

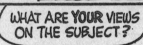

HAVE YOU EVER TRIED TO WRITE WITH A PEN, LINUS?

I'VE BEEN PRACTICING FOR A WEEK NOW, AND I THINK I'M GETTING BETTER...HERE, TRY IT..

DON'T BE WORRIED IF YOU DO POORLY AT FIRST....YOU'LL PROBABLY HAVE THE SAME TROUBLE THAT I....

Dear Pen-pal,
How are you?

THIS IS AN INTERESTING ARTICLE

IT SAYS THAT TV IS NOT HARMFUL TO CHILDREN..

DO YOU THINK TV IS HARMFUL TO YOU, LINUS?

I DON'T KNOW...I'VE NEVER HAD ONE FALL ON ME!

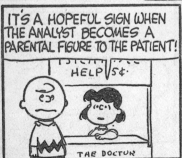

WHAT DOES MISS OTHMAR THINK ABOUT YOUR BRINGING THAT BLANKET TO SCHOOL?

SHE DOESN'T LIKE IT SO I'M TRYING TO GET HER TO MAKE AN AGREEMENT WITH ME...

I TOLD HER I'D GIVE UP MY BLANKET IF SHE'D GIVE UP BITING HER FINGERNAILS...

WHAT DID SHE SAY TO THAT?

I COULDN'T TELL... SHE HAD HER HEAD DOWN ON THE DESK!

YOU WHAT?

I MADE AN AGREEMENT WITH MISS OTHMAR... I'LL GIVE UP MY BLANKET IF SHE CAN GIVE UP BITING HER FINGERNAILS!

I HAVE A FEELING YOU DON'T THINK SHE CAN DO IT...

POOR MISS OTHMAR..

HEE HEE HEE HEE HEE

WHAT A SITUATION..

MISS OTHMAR IS GOING TO PROVE TO LINUS THAT YOU CAN BREAK A HABIT WITH SHEER WILL POWER SO SHE'S GOING TO STOP BITING HER FINGERNAILS

LINUS IS SO SURE THAT SHE CAN'T DO IT HE'S RISKING HIS BELOVED BLANKET..

IN THESE TEACHER-PUPIL STRUGGLES IT'S ALWAYS THE PRINCIPAL WHO LOSES!

WHAT IN THE WORLD....?..

I'M SURRENDERING... I'M GOING TO MISS OTHMAR ON MY HANDS AND KNEES TO SURRENDER...

I GOTTA HAVE MY BLANKET BACK...I CAN'T GO ON LIKE THIS...DO I LOOK HUMBLE?

NAUSEATINGLY HUMBLE!!

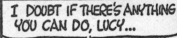

I PROMISED CHARLIE BROWN THAT I'D TRY TO TALK TO YOU, SCHROEDER..

NOW, LET'S BE PRACTICAL ABOUT THIS THING..WHO MAKES THE MOST MONEY, A CONCERT PIANIST OR A BASEBALL CATCHER?

A CONCERT PIANIST!

WHAT'S THE MATTER WITH YOU CHARLIE BROWN? WHY DON'T YOU LEAVE SCHROEDER ALONE?!

"WANT ADS" ALWAYS GET RESULTS, CHARLIE BROWN...

WE'LL PHONE YOUR AD IN TO THE PAPER REQUESTING A JOB AS MANAGER OF A BALL CLUB, AND I'LL BET YOU'LL BE FLOODED WITH OFFERS!

"WANT ADS" ARE FAMOUS FOR BEING ABLE TO SELL ANYTHING

I FEEL LIKE AN OLD SEWING MACHINE!